Strategic Sustainability

Why it Matters to Your Business and How to Make It Happen

T0298874

Alexandra McKay

M4C

e: alex@m4c-sustainability.co.uk

w: www.m4c-sustainability.co.uk

bl: m4c-sustainability.co.uk/blog

tw: m4c_sust

First published in 2013 by Dō Sustainability
87 Lonsdale Road, Oxford OX2 7ET, UK

ISBN 978-1-909293-55-7 (eBook-ePub)
ISBN 978-1-909293-56-4 (eBook-PDF)
ISBN 978-1-909293-54-0 (Paperback)

A catalogue record for this title is available from the British Library.

Dō Sustainability strives for net positive social and environmental impact. See our sustainability policy at **www.dosustainability.com**.

Page design and typesetting by Alison Rayner
Cover by Becky Chilcott

For further information on Dō Sustainability, visit our website:
www.dosustainability.com

DōShorts

Dō Sustainability is the publisher of **DōShorts**: short, high-value ebooks that distil sustainability best practice and business insights for busy, results-driven professionals. Each DōShort can be read in 90 minutes.

New and forthcoming DōShorts – stay up to date

We publish 3 to 5 new DōShorts each month. The best way to keep up to date? Sign up to our short, monthly newsletter. Go to **www. dosustainability.com/newsletter** to sign up to the Dō Newsletter. Some of our latest and forthcoming titles include:

- *The First 100 Days on the Job: How to Plan, Prioritise & Build a Sustainable Organisation*   Anne Augustine
- *Full Product Transparency: Cutting the Fluff Out of Sustainability*   Ramon Arratia
- *Making the Most of Standards*   Adrian Henriques
- *How to Account for Sustainability: A Business Guide to Measuring and Managing*   Laura Musikanski
- *Sustainability in the Public Sector: An Essential Briefing for Stakeholders*   Sonja Powell
- *Sustainability Reporting for SMEs: Competitive Advantage Through Transparency*   Elaine Cohen
- *REDD+ and Business Sustainability: A Guide to Reversing Deforestation for Forward Thinking Companies*   Brian McFarland
- *How Gamification Can Help Your Business Engage in Sustainability*   Paula Owen
- *Sustainable Energy Options for Business*   Philip Wolfe

- *Adapting to Climate Change: 2.0 Enterprise Risk Management*
  Mark Trexler & Laura Kosloff

- *How to Engage Youth to Drive Corporate Sustainability: Roles and Interventions*   Nicolò Wojewoda

- *The Short Guide to Sustainable Investing*   Cary Krosinsky

Subscriptions

In addition to individual sales of our ebooks, we now offer subscriptions. Access 60+ ebooks for the price of 5 with a personal subscription to our full e-library. Institutional subscriptions are also available for your staff or students. Visit **www.dosustainability.com/books/subscriptions** or email **veruschka@dosustainability.com**

Write for us, or suggest a DōShort

Please visit **www.dosustainability.com** for our full publishing programme. If you don't find what you need, write for us! Or suggest a DōShort on our website. We look forward to hearing from you.

....

Abstract

IN MANY BUSINESSES sustainability is often one person's passion and responsibility. A large part of their job becomes selling sustainability to other people in the business, people who may have the power to do something about it or people who are the decision-makers. This book sets out why sustainability is of strategic importance to businesses, why action is essential to them and how sustainability can help them not only survive but thrive in competitive marketplaces. The book outlines some of the key reasons why and how businesses that are not multinationals should take action on sustainability. It looks in detail at some of the key issues and why they are of strategic importance to businesses, including how to integrate and link sustainability strategy with business strategy and mission. The book offers guidance on gaining buy-in from key decision-makers and actors in a business to move a sustainability programme on and make a real, positive impact – on business, society and the environment.

About the Author

 **ALEXANDRA MCKAY** has worked for M4C, a leading sustainability consultancy with a strong focus on communications, since 2007. In that time she has worked with a variety of companies – from multinationals to SMEs – on all aspects of their sustainability programmes including strategy development and implementation, reporting, supply chain management and systems implementation.

....

Contents

CONTENTS

CHAPTER 1

Why Sustainability Matters to Your Business

PEOPLE AND BUSINESSES GET INVOLVED in sustainability for very different reasons.

Generally, individuals are emotionally or morally driven to act – to improve or protect the world for their and their children's future. This may be a long-term concern or something triggered more recently – an epiphany moment – caused by something they have seen or experienced. Whatever their concern or why they feel driven to act, it is fair to say that they believe taking action to make our world fairer and more sustainable is the right thing to do.

While they may not use the terms themselves, they believe we have a moral obligation to take action. While these motivations make perfect sense for individuals, the same cannot be said for businesses. Businesses may just be a collection of individuals, but hierarchy and bureaucracy require very different motivations to change or take action.

Large-scale changes have been made to businesses because of one person's epiphany moment – for example, that of the late Ray Anderson, Founder and Chairman of Interface FLOR – but more often a sound business case and strategic purpose is required. In the face of business's primary aim – and legal and moral obligation – to protect and enhance shareholder value, 'it's the right thing to do' does not carry much weight.

This book will help you develop a business case to convince the most sceptical Finance Officer or Chief Executive Officer that sustainability can offer real value to a business.

First, we need to understand what makes businesses tick and how sustainability can help deliver that. From saving money in operations or production, attracting new customers, retaining existing customers, protecting and improving brand, sustainability can help.

What is sustainability?

Definitions of sustainability in a business context do vary. I am taking the broader view of balancing and enhancing the social, environmental and economic sustainability of the business. This is also known as the triple bottom line, referring to a business's economic, environmental and social impacts, summarised as the three Ps – People, Planet, Profit.

Some businesses take a narrower view of sustainability, focusing just on environmental issues, and perhaps include their community investment or health and safety activities. I prefer the broader view, as it represents the full spectrum of risks and opportunities open to businesses, and really gets to the heart of what it takes to make a business successful over the long term.

For the sceptic

So what if the above doesn't apply to you? You've had no epiphany moment, and this sustainability stuff has been dumped on you by an enthusiastic manager.

The purpose of this book is to help you get started; to explain the benefits of sustainability and build a business case. I hope at least some of it will ring true and you will finish a little less sceptical than you began and a little more convinced that sustainability can bring real benefits to your business. I will show that this isn't some ridiculous fad but a sensible approach to doing business. I'm sure you will find that your business is tackling many of the issues to a greater or lesser extent. I'm convinced that by thinking about sustainability in a strategic way you can reap more benefits and transform your business into a leaner and more flexible organisation, and more environmentally, socially and economically sustainable.

Steps

To develop and implement a sustainability programme into your business you need resources, both people and money. Unfortunately, to convince people and get those resources, you need to have an idea of what it is you can do – itself a process which may require people and money. In many ways this is back-to-front as once your team is in place you will want to go through the same process in greater depth using their experience and input. The things you need to have a good grasp of before you begin are:

1. Why the issues matter generally.

2. At a high level, the issues that are material to your business.

3. The resources you are likely to need – both people and money.

4. Understanding your business, business objectives and audience.

5. Making the case.

6. Developing a strategy.

7. How to implement it!

In this Dō Short we'll be focusing mostly on steps 1–5.

Benefits: Why sustainability matters...

You'll soon find that sustainability takes effort and input from all kinds of people from both inside and outside your business. It is important to understand how and why your sustainability programme matters to these groups and how taking action can benefit your business.

... Operationally

When first looking at sustainability most companies look to their operations and specifically the savings that can be made. More often than not there are many quick wins to be made; costs are easy to see and measure; and the changes are more or less under the business's control.

Obviously, the operational savings that can be made vary greatly from company to company and industry to industry. However, the principles are broadly the same:

Saving money: Many of the world's resources are finite and yet we are often totally reliant on them, oil in particular. You are probably aware of the idea of peak oil, the point where oil production reduces as a result of reduced reserves, making it more difficult to extract and therefore more expensive. Oil is obviously essential to our daily lives as a source of energy and in the production of many materials. While the idea of peak oil is quite common other resources are also becoming scarcer. Warnings have been made about the supply of helium, for example, which, other than filling balloons, has a number of uses including medically in magnetic resonance imaging (MRI) machines and in leak detection.

If we are to be sustainable we need to reduce our reliance on these materials, and do more with less. The joy of this is that it will save you money: by printing on both sides of a piece of paper you need to buy less paper; by switching things off when you don't need them you save electricity, reduce your energy bills and your carbon footprint; if your staff travel less they use less fuel and reduce unproductive travel time. To begin with at least, it's very simple. Although once you've picked this low-hanging fruit some capital investment may be needed to see further reductions.

How do you start identifying where savings can be made? Energy, water and waste tend to be good starting points – just ask what can get switched off, where can we use less, what don't we need to use or buy? With waste don't just think about segregation. Most of what you throw away you bought at some point, so can you reduce waste higher up the chain by not buying it in the first place? Or is there a more sustainable, cost-effective alternative?

Look at your costs. The places where you spend generally give the greatest opportunity for savings. Walk through your operations, looking at and questioning everything. Tip: don't make yourself too annoying, as you'll want these people on your side later.

Making money: Sustainability isn't just about savings. The three pillars are environment/society/economic or people/planet/profit. Sustainability gives each equal weight and is about balancing all three. After all, you can't be a sustainable business without making money.

Generating your own renewable energy is one way of making money out of your sustainability programme and helping you reduce your carbon footprint at the same time. Many businesses have also found that by segregating their waste they can make money selling it on to waste handlers – quite a turnaround from escalating landfill taxes. But for most businesses that is always going to be a sideline with the primary goal of reducing overheads. The real trick is identifying ways to make your existing products more sustainable and then developing tailored sustainable products. This could mean incorporating a sustainable aspect into your existing products by, for example, using more sustainable materials in the production of your components; incorporating recycled materials; or gaining some accreditation, which are as diverse as energy star (which recognises lower energy electronics) to fairtrade.

As well as products that are themselves more sustainable, you should also look at ways they can help make your customers more sustainable. This could include reducing the energy use of your products or offering organic, fairtrade, FSC (Forest Stewardship Council) products or environmentally-friendly options such as low emission or hybrid vehicles.

Services are a little more tricky, but it is still possible. This could include diversifying to offer a sustainable option, such as fitting renewable energy sources; offering 'carbon-neutral' services; helping companies use their equipment more efficiently; using the most efficient and sustainable processes available, such as water-free printing or offering ethical investments.

Whatever you do, sustainability can help you sell and market your product or service, or if you develop tailored sustainable products, even tap into a new market. Sustainability could be the thing that sways a potential customer to choose you.

... To your employees

Hopefully you realise how vital your employees are to your business; they develop and deliver your products or services, can be your biggest advocates, interact with your customers, and ensure you remain compliant with legislation.

So why does sustainability matter to them? As a large part of sustainability is about managing your key relationships, it could help you manage how you interact with your employees. Once again sustainability sits on a convergence of interests. To operate sustainably you need safe, healthy, trained, happy, motivated employees. All of which your employees appreciate, too, and will make them want to stay with you and be more committed to the business.

Many individuals are looking for ways in which they can meet their life goals. So businesses that offer the opportunity for employees to do this in the workplace will ensure a more engaged workforce. This is highlighted by the fact that many companies report lower recruitment costs due to their sustainability programme. People like and want to work for a nice, responsible company, so are more likely to stay. And it makes it easier to find and recruit talented people from the start as people will choose to work for you. In fact, research by BT showed that 44% of young professionals would avoid working for an employer that showed poor social responsibility, while more than a third thought that working for a responsible employer was more important to them than the salary they earned.[1]

Many years ago, when I was Secretary of State for the Environment, Unilever came to see me with, what was then, an amazing series of environmental innovations and business systems which were utterly new. At the end of their presentation I asked them, what surprised you about it? Their response was that they had paid for it all through recruitment and retention. By making their business more responsible they attracted the best graduates, and kept them. When you consider the cost of recruitment and retention, both very expensive; Unilever believed the savings they had made paid for the innovative roll out of their environmental programme.

John Selwyn Gummer, Baron Deben

... To your customers

As with all these things, your product or service, and who you supply it to, will determine your key issues. But as a general rule, sustainability is something your customers will be interested in and something they will be looking for in a supplier.

Let's be honest here; sustainability isn't going to be, and shouldn't be, the only thing your customers are looking for. The usual factors like costs, experience and quality will always, and should always, play a part; remember that the economic pillar is important. But sustainability provides an additional advantage that could be the difference between whether or not that potential customer becomes an actual customer.

If you're lucky, sustainability might make you stand out in your field. If you're less lucky a lack of focus on sustainability can also make you stand out, but for all the wrong reasons. If you are supplying to a large company or to the public sector, they are very aware that their supply chain is seen as a reflection of them and their values. If one of their suppliers is seen or found to be doing something untoward, the media, their customers and the general public hold them responsible. If you are taking action on sustainability it reassures them that you are managing your risks and reputation, which therefore reduces the risks to their business and reputation.

Public sector: If you supply into the public sector you have probably noticed that sustainability, and ISO 14001 in particular, is increasingly becoming a requirement. If you haven't already, speak to your sales team and the people who fill in tenders and see what they think.

You will see very few 'Invitation to Tender' documents or 'Pre-qualification Questionnaires' without a sustainability, or at the very least an environment, section. Even if sustainability is not specifically mentioned in a tender document, being able to talk about your sustainability activities will always be seen by public sector buyers as adding value and acting as a differentiator. In fact, the Social Value Act 2012 means that public authorities will have to consider social and environmental well-being in public services contracts and not just make decisions based on cost.

Given the time and effort involved in tendering, is sustainability really a hurdle you want to fall at?

Private sector: Most FTSE 100 companies in the UK now produce a sustainability report. While, in reality, commitment varies, a good proportion of them will be looking to work with or partner with businesses that share their values.

Partnering is increasingly a focus, with companies recognising the value and expertise their suppliers can and do bring to their business. While you may not directly supply a FTSE-sized company, you are likely to be in their supply chain. Even if you aren't, the focus on sustainability is being replicated across the corporate world – the fact you are even reading this Short shows something.

Businesses are increasingly aware of the reputational risks associated with their supply chain, so taking positive action to implement a sustainability programme provides them with reassurance that you are a safe company to work with. If you can provide a product or service contributing to their sustainability efforts that they can then brag about in their sustainability report, then all the better!

General public: If the general public buy your product or service, things get a little more complicated.

People are aware of and care about sustainability and green issues. A YouGov survey found that 73% of British citizens consider sustainable living to be important to them,[2] and 70% of Asda customers said that they care a lot about green issues.[3] When asked in surveys, people overwhelmingly say that sustainability influences their buying decisions. However, in reality this is true of a niche group; the rest are just as swayed by price, quality and various other factors. However, they do *just* expect companies to be doing something – and if you are proven to fail they may turn away. The bottom line is that it can't hurt to be doing something but it may hurt not to be, or worse if it turns out you (or your suppliers) are doing something which could be seen as bad. Those companies identified as paying no corporation tax in the UK were not doing anything illegal but it didn't stop the harm to their public image. But it does in a large part depend on who you are, what you are selling and to whom.

... To your community

It may or may not come as a surprise to discover that businesses do not exist in isolation from the rest of society. Your employees, suppliers and neighbours are all people who are part of society and communities, whether or not they are geographically close to your business. Your product, service or operations will directly or indirectly impact these people and by extension their communities. What needs to be managed is whether these impacts are positive or negative.

People in communities talk to each other and share information and opinions, which are potentially about your company. If people say and think positive things about your company that generates goodwill. This makes your employees happier – people like to work for a good company; your customers more likely to buy from you; it could make your neighbours less likely to complain. This is all difficult to measure and quantify but makes a real difference to your business. It is one of the foundations of that most valuable business asset – your reputation. To quote Warren Buffett, 'It takes 20 years to build a reputation and five minutes to ruin it.'

Your sustainability activities can help generate goodwill and a positive reputation. All your sustainability activities can help, from the obvious support of community groups and charities to neighbours feeling better about your site because you're managing noise and other pollution to the kudos that comes with the sustainability label stamped on your packaging or e-signatures. A sustainability programme can also help generate positive PR, as you tell the story of your best practice initiative or are lauded as an industry leader. Difficult to measure – but invaluable.

... To your regulators

So much of what is becoming legislation started out as a niche corporate responsibility or sustainability activity, from carbon management and reduction to packaging regulations, and this doesn't seem likely to be a trend that will be bucked any time soon. So from your perspective, a well managed sustainability programme can help you not only stay on the right side of regulations but also stay one step ahead of the regulators.

Regulators will be pleased because you can demonstrate you are remaining within the spirit as well as the letter of the law, which can only help your relationship. Industries that are voluntarily taking action on sustainability issues may also avoid additional regulatory burdens.

... In your supply chain

You may question why you should or need to work with your suppliers. I think there are three good reasons:

Security: Particularly if you produce something physical, ensuring a secure supply of your component parts or materials is essential, as is knowing where they come from. There have been numerous examples recently of poor supply chain management coming back to bite companies.

Following the Japanese earthquake in 2011 many companies suddenly discovered that a key component originated from Japan. Had they known this component came from Japan, they may have been able to put contingencies in place to manage it. As it happened they didn't and they weren't able to be proactive in finding an alternative source or manage the supply gap. So purely from a business continuity perspective, understanding your supply chain is vital. While this is an extreme example, changes in climate, freak weather events, and even political unrest can put your supply chain at risk.

Reputation and responsibility: Like it or not an issue in your supply chain can reflect badly on you, even if you think it is outside of your control. The recent horsemeat debacle shows how long, disjointed, anonymous supply chains can land companies in trouble.

Clothing chains have also been lambasted for their suppliers' behaviour, even for activities in their tier-two supply chain. The BBC *Panorama* documentary, 'Primark: On the Rack'[4] is one example of this. Primark were vilified for activities in their tier-two supply chain which were being intentionally hidden from them. Despite their swift action, the company were held responsible and heavily criticised by the media, causing severe reputational damage, despite the fact the BBC later apologised over some of the programme's content.

It is no longer acceptable to live in blissful ignorance of what is happening in your supply chain – your stakeholders will expect you to know about and be influencing your suppliers' behaviour.

Partnership: But it isn't all bad news. Suppliers are often depicted as lax, irresponsible and ignorant of sustainability. What you are likely to find in your supply chain is a variety of companies at varying stages of their sustainability journey.

There are some you may be able to help on their way but there will be some who can help you. This could be with their knowledge or experience; with a new or alternative product or service that they didn't think you'd be interested in; or with a new way of working. There are also savings to be made; by working together, consolidating or sharing, you can save money and reduce your impact.

However you choose to work with your suppliers, chances are they will be keen to develop a closer, mutually beneficial relationship with you, their customer.

Summary

In summary, actively managing sustainability in your operations brings a variety of benefits to your business, various stakeholders and the environment. For your business a sustainability programme can:

- reduce costs
- increase sales and give you access to new markets
- improve business resilience
- improve staff motivation
- ensure legal compliance
- contribute to the efficient running of the business
- build and improve your reputation

QUESTIONS AND ACTIONS

- What groups does your business impact?
- Which relationships could be improved?
- What are the key arguments that will make an impact in your business?

CHAPTER 2

Identifying Your Material Issues

SO NOW WE HAVE AN UNDERSTANDING of why sustainability matters to your business and your stakeholders, the next step is to identify your key business impact areas, or material issues.

Let's start with a definition: sustainability can, like all business trends, be chock-full of buzz words for relatively straightforward ideas. Material issues are the areas where your business has, or could potentially have, the biggest sustainability impacts on people and the planet.

So how do we identify them? This won't be, and shouldn't be, a final list; it should be a high level idea of your material issues to provide a framework and some guidance. This will help position sustainability in discussions and when engaging various groups.

Draw a picture or take a walk

Your material issues are based on what your business actually does – what you buy, who you buy it from, any processes involved, what you sell, who you sell it to and the impacts of all of that on communities and the environment.

Thinking about all of that is vital, and thinking about it afresh just as much so. So draw yourself a diagram or flow chart of your business operations, or go for a walk around your site (stick your nose into as many forgotten nooks and crannies as possible), look at what comes in and what goes out – and see your business and its impacts on people and the planet with fresh eyes.

Ask people

Also known as stakeholder engagement, talking to people both inside and outside your organisation about what they see as the biggest issues for your business is a great way to find out your stakeholders priorities and how they see your business.

It is also a great opportunity to see your business from a different perspective. While you are fretting over the sustainability of a key component of your product, your customer may be more concerned about the excess packaging. This may not cover everything and may prove contradictory – a stakeholder may have a particular axe to grind so will have a definite agenda, while customers and investors will have very different outlooks, but it will help you develop your priorities. Look at complaints, from customers, regulators and neighbours, in particular; it may not be pretty but it will be honest.

You may find that the material issues that are of greatest concern to your stakeholders may not be the biggest issues for your business. This doesn't mean they are wrong and you can ignore them. Small things can make a huge difference, even if it is just in someone's perception of your business, especially if your largest impacts and actions are hidden from view in your supply chain. Small things like office recycling give cues to the behaviour expected elsewhere. So when you are deciding on your focus areas, think about the overall impression you want to give and what is important to your stakeholders as well as where you have the largest impacts.

Follow the money

Money has an impact, for good or ill, so it stands to reason that businesses have an impact where they spend or make money. Look at the people and environment wherever you buy from and sell to, as well as what you buy and sell and what it is made from. Look at where you spend (and make) large amounts of money; if you spend a lot on energy, for example, it is likely your carbon footprint will be large.

If your profits are derived from a particular demographic, how are they affected, what issues are they facing and how does your product or service affect them?

Risks

What areas has the business already identified as risk areas? Sustainability is about the economic sustainability of your business as much as social and environmental. Looking at pre-existing risks and how sustainability can help will not only help to make your business more sustainable, it will help to convince the right people, too.

Business risks often have impacts or origins beyond your office walls or factory gates. If you're struggling to recruit people with the right skills in an area of high unemployment there are obvious ways you can tie a high risk area in with a community investment activity, providing benefits to your business and the local community. If the business is concerned about rising energy costs there are clear ways a strategic approach to sustainability can help.

Motivation

Why are you reading this? What started your organisation on their sustainability journey? Knowing the motivation behind this will help to identify why a sustainability programme, or a particular aspect of a sustainability programme, is of strategic importance to your business.

Some motivations may be transparent and require no unravelling – 'we're paying too much to dispose of our waste/for electricity/on fuel' are all fairly easy to understand and tackle. Motivations related to reputation or recruitment and retention may be more difficult to unpick, may not be as straightforward as they seem and may have multiple causes. However, they will still give you a good indication of where to look and possibly which stakeholders to engage.

If your motivations do relate to the external perception of your business you need to ensure external communication forms a part of your strategy.

What are your competitors doing?

If your competitors already have an established sustainability programme, look with interest at what they have identified as their material issues – don't copy but be inspired by what is happening in your marketplace, not only by what is being done well, but by what is being done badly. As well as seeing what a similar company has identified as material, look at where your competitors are missing a trick. Based on this, think about your strengths: where can you carve out a niche for yourself and what could become your sustainability unique selling point (USP).

It may also be useful to look beyond your competitors to your customers and supply chain. What have they identified as their material issues and is there any overlap with your business?

Standards

Looking at what standards are available and are commonly used or expected in your industry and beyond, can be a useful way to meet stakeholder expectations and demonstrate your programme is well managed. It can also help you to get an idea of the resources you will need.

ISO 14001 is the most common certification for environmental management systems across all industries, although others exist such as EMAS. ISO 14001 or a similar certification is often requested on tender documents as a sign a company is managing their environmental impacts. OHAS 18001 is similarly used to certify health and safety management systems.

There are also standards that accredit your carbon footprint, such as CFV Carbon Footprint Verification or the Carbon Trust Standard; your product's lifecycle carbon footprint such as PAS 2050; community investment, such as the London Benchmarking Group; industry specific standards, such as ISO 20121 Sustainable Events Management; or your whole approach to sustainability, such as the BitC CR index or ISO 26000 guidelines for social responsibility.

All of these come at a cost so you need to budget for them. Some are designed to work together, for example, ISO 14001 and OHAS 18001, so it may make sense to implement the two at the same time, or build on existing systems.

Stop thinking about it and do something

Many people fall into the trap of trying to think of every possible issue that could affect their business and trying to organise them in the ideal, most logical way. As a result they don't do anything other than shuffle pieces of paper around and generally get more and more confused.

Sustainability programmes are large, multi-issue, cross-departmental and quite complicated. As a result, getting a handle on them and finding a concise way to communicate them is always a challenge. However, you don't have to get it right first time. Your sustainability programme will grow and evolve as your approach and business changes and develops. You will find that companies that have been looking at sustainability for many years will have changed their approach, their priorities and their way of organising it a number of times in that time.

At the end of the day, if you don't take action you will never get any of the benefits a sustainability programme will bring. It is far better to make a start and discover a little way down the road that you missed something or have included something that, in retrospect, isn't quite so vital than never to make a start.

QUESTIONS AND ACTIONS

- Take a walk around your site
- What issues do you think are most material to the business?
- What is your business's biggest expenditure?
- What standards are relevant and most used in your industry?
- What are your competitors, customers and suppliers doing?
- Who does the company sell to and what issues are they facing?
- Whose opinions are you going to ask?

CHAPTER 3

Identify Resources

UNFORTUNATELY, SUSTAINABILITY CAN'T BE DONE by one person; if it could, more companies would be doing more and doing it better.

Getting the right people is key to successfully implementing a sustainability programme.

The people you need will ideally have three things:

- **Authority:** to make the necessary decisions and changes. Things may – and should – be stamped or authorised by the relevant management but your team needs some authority to usefully influence, change processes and alter the direction of things in your business.

- **Knowledge:** you, as an individual, aren't expected to be an expert on every aspect of sustainability or your business. In fact, you may not have in-depth knowledge on any aspect of the sustainability programme and instead just bring together the different strands and manage the implementation process. Instead, your team should bring the in-depth knowledge of different aspects of your business, from how the widgets are made and why they are done like that, to how your company's purchasing process works.

- **Enthusiasm:** possibly the hardest to find and often the most useful.

Working with enthusiastic people who 'get' sustainability, what you are trying to do, the reasons behind it and are enthusiastic about it, can make the whole process easier, move more smoothly and generally be more pleasant.

You may not get all three of these qualities in every individual on your team but getting a good mix and having all three represented within your team is key.

External help

While you as an individual aren't expected to be an expert on every aspect of sustainability or your business, neither are your team. You will find that external support is available on all aspects of your programme, from strategy development or environmental management systems to resource efficiency or community investment. You may also find sustainability experts who specialise in your specific industry. Some outside assistance may be invaluable, whether it is just to get your programme moving or to help you find and make big savings.

Obviously external help can come at a cost and can be very expensive. Most companies will use a select group of sustainability suppliers based on their needs, time, budget, internal expertise and material issues.

There is good news. Despite these straitened economic times, free support is still available, particularly relating to resource efficiency. This tends to be provided on a regional basis, and you may need to meet certain criteria, for example, free support may only be available for SMEs, but it is worth a quick internet search or phone call to your local chamber of commerce, council or Groundwork team.

QUESTIONS AND ACTIONS

- Which departments or areas will need to be involved?

- Can you identify any skills or knowledge gaps that will require external assistance?

CHAPTER 4

Issues You May Look At – and How to Link Them to Your Business

SO FAR THIS HAS BEEN VERY THEORETICAL, so what might a sustainability programme in your business actually look like? It's a good idea to have some answers as it is a question people are bound to ask. Here are some examples of how other companies have tackled certain issues well.

Create a USP

First, a word of warning. Don't think you can or should do everything straight away. Instead, think about creating your sustainability niche or USP. This should be based on your biggest impact areas, biggest risks, perhaps what you are already doing well or what your competitors are doing badly. In other words, focus on a handful of areas that you do, or could do, really well.

Resource efficiency: energy, water, waste

Many companies begin their sustainability journey by looking at resource efficiency. It is easy to see, measure and achieve savings with very little financial outlay. It is also easy to see the benefit to the business and in particular to the bottom line.

As a result there are lots of good case studies available, but few companies make resource efficiency their sustainability USP. One exception is Interface FLOR, whose CEO had a famous epiphany moment which totally changed the direction of the company.[5] He transformed the business based on the principles of sustainability and learning from nature and a desire to be fully sustainable and have zero negative impact. The company set out to eliminate waste by recycling and reusing materials and improving energy and transport efficiency, among other initiatives.

In road resurfacing, companies have developed techniques to recycle the old surface in situ to create the new road surface. If you can't reuse your own waste then look into the possibility of selling your waste on – it's not a new idea after all, with marmite being based on a by-product from the brewing industry. The National Industrial Symbiosis Programme works to link companies together who can provide or use waste materials.

Other companies have saved millions through saved materials by reducing their packaging – for example, the weight of their drinks cans. Other companies have improved the efficiency of their vehicle fleets by buying more efficient vehicles and training drivers to drive more safely and efficiently and saving money on fuel costs.

Energy reduction is an area where many companies can make significant savings. The simplest solution, which is to switch things off or down when they aren't in use, costs nothing depending on levels of control. Smart metering is useful to identify problem areas. Most resource efficiency consultants have tales of single offices using twice as much energy as their neighbours because the occupants had turned the thermostat or air conditioning up as they preferred a warmer/cooler room. That said, some energy saving solutions do require some financial outlay.

Switching equipment off is all very well but if you need a large number of people, for example, to switch their computers or lights off, a behaviour change campaign can be quite intensive and difficult to get right. There are solutions available to reduce or remove the need for this kind of intervention, such as building management systems or movement responsive lighting. But while upgrading to more efficient equipment – from LED lighting to new machinery – may have a financial outlay it can also have short payback periods.

The lateral thinking with resource efficiency comes when working with neighbours and partners. Companies have come to agreements where, for example, excess heat generated by a company's processes or machinery is used by their neighbour to warm their greenhouses or where haulage competitors have worked together to share loads and reduce empty road miles.

Carbon and renewables

Carbon reduction often goes hand in hand with energy and transport efficiency. The extra steps come with climate adaptation, renewable energy and measurement.

Climate adaptation is about improving business resilience to climate related risks. This could be ensuring the security of key food ingredients which may be affected by water scarcity or other impacts of climate change. It could also be the insurance industry developing and adapting products which manage the risks associated with, or deal with, extreme weather events.

With renewable energy many companies produce their own renewable energy on-site. This ranges from solar panels to a community anaerobic digester. Other companies have committed to source all their electricity from renewable sources via their electricity provider.

Carbon measurement can be used to good effect to highlight the strategic importance of carbon. Walkers conducted an in-depth product carbon lifecycle assessment.[6] As a result they are able to print the carbon footprint on the back of their packets of crisps.

Your product or service

Aligning and embedding sustainability into your product or service is one of the trickiest and most company specific parts of your sustainability programme. However, it is also one of the most worthwhile, and is necessary to transform your business into a truly sustainable business. There is very little point in having carbon neutral operations if you send your product out into the world to pollute or quickly be resigned to landfill.

The first step is to understand your product or service lifecycle including its packaging, identifying where the largest impacts are and targeting your attentions there. This takes time and effort and possibly specialist help.

This may also be influenced by your approach to sustainability and your sustainability USP. It should also meet your customers' requirements and demands – after all, there is no point developing a sustainable product that no-one wants.

It may be about reducing the energy consumption of the electronics you produce; expanding your product range to include eco-technologies such as renewables or insulation; offering a sustainable alternative, such as a line of sustainably sourced fish products; ensuring the packaging of your product is minimal and recyclable. For services, you may start fitting renewables or insulation; offering carbon off-setting for your service; offering services which help your customer reduce their impacts, such as video-conferencing; or offering ethical investments.

Human rights

Many companies don't want to admit to having issues with human rights so examples are often buried or highly edited. However, there are still some examples of companies that have embraced the human rights challenges facing their businesses and supply chains.

Fairtrade is one example of businesses working positively to ensure human rights are respected in their supply chain. Others use alternative means to tackle problem areas. One example is SABMiller who were trying to stop parents at their sugar plantation in Honduras from bringing their children to work with them. Instead of telling them to leave their children at home, potentially alone, they provided a school for the children to attend while their parents were at work.[7]

Supply chain

Working with your supply chain tends to be an extension of the issues affecting the business itself. Large companies tend to have more success when working with their supply chain as they have greater buying power and therefore greater sway.

A number of companies, particularly retailers with large supply chains, have had great success developing supply networks. The networks allow the company to engage their suppliers in sustainability issues or in a particular issue and often give the opportunity of peer-to-peer sharing of best practice, etc. This close networking often includes the sharing of any benefits and cost savings.

Other supply chain initiatives deal with specific business issues. Faced with an aging population of cocoa farmers, Cadbury has taken action working with their cocoa growers in Ghana to ensure the future of their supply.[8] Their Cadbury Cocoa Partnership funds research and invests in farming communities, making cocoa farming a more attractive proposition to the next generation. For smaller companies this may be buying local produce or from local suppliers, choosing lower impact goods or working with suppliers to minimise excess packaging.

Community

Most businesses have some kind of community investment programme or support charities through donations. What fewer do is have a strategic approach to community investment. This tends to involve closer working between the business and the charity or community group and generally brings benefits to both sides of the relationship.

Manchester Airport's Airport Academy is one great example of this kind of working. The academy delivers training and work experience to unemployed people from the local area as a first step to working at the airport. The programme ensures employers at the airport have access to people with the right skills and provides people from the local area with employment and skills.[9]

Other companies use community investment and employee volunteering to develop employees' skills. Allianz Insurance use volunteering to help employees develop communication and leadership skills and deliver valuable services to their partner charities.[10]

Employees and labour issues

A sustainability programme can cover a wide range of employee issues including training, pay and working conditions, diversity and health and safety.

In industries where low pay is a concern some companies have committed to pay their staff a living wage. Where work/life balance is a concern companies have developed a variety of best practice tools to support staff. This includes stress management initiatives, flexible working and teleconferencing and telecommuting.

Effective training can prove invaluable for employers and employees. Companies' approach to training includes setting targets for average training levels, setting up internal training academies, identifying training routes to leadership roles and using volunteering as a skills development tool as highlighted above.

Diversity can be a challenging issue to deal with, with many companies reticent to set targets in this area. Instead, companies have delivered diversity training to all employees and those specifically involved in recruitment decisions. Some companies have also looked at where they hire from to ensure they are not creating unnecessary barriers.

Health and safety is a core priority for many businesses. As a result many companies have developed flagship programmes to help reduce the number and seriousness of accidents. Training and awareness are core to reducing accident rates so most successful health and safety campaigns are built around these elements.

Many companies also run well-being campaigns. These focus on potential health and well-being issues affecting employees outside their work environment. This can be highlighting the benefits of an active lifestyle and healthy diet, smoking cessation, early identification of illnesses such as heart disease or skin cancer, or tailored to the demographic of the workforce such as a focus on men's or women's health. Many companies also focus on helping their employees manage their work/life balance and deal with stress.

QUESTIONS AND ACTIONS

- What is the business already doing and what issues are already being looked at?

- What could/does it do well?

- Which areas will be the easiest sell?

- Which areas will be the hardest to sell?

- What are companies in your value chain doing?

CHAPTER 5

How to Make it Happen

Selling sustainability

SO WE NOW HAVE A BROAD UNDERSTANDING of why sustainability may be of strategic importance to your business, why it matters to a variety of stakeholders and some idea of what you are likely to need to do. The next job is to make it happen.

Don't start by developing a strategy; you need to do that later with the input of others in your business. Instead, what you need is a sound business case, which, like all good sales pitches, can be tailored to your audience.

The key is to get your key players on board. Unfortunately, sustainability can't be done by one person and you need to get buy-in from across the business. Let's not beat around the bush here – developing and implementing a company-wide sustainability programme is going to take time and money. And, unless your business is very unusual, I'd guess both of these resources are in limited supply.

You need to think about who you need to convince; what motivates them; how will it benefit them; what you need from them; and whether you need any additional resources or funds.

Before you start

Before you start developing your business case and start trying to convince various people you need to make sure that you understand and are familiar with a few things:

- The basics and benefits of sustainability

- A high-level idea of the material issues affecting your business

- A good understanding of your business, in particular:
  - Business risks
  - Business strategy
  - Company mission and values
  - Any results from staff or customer surveys
  - What the company actually sells
  - Where the money comes from
  - Why your customers choose to buy from you
  - What the key motivations for change are

- A list of requirements and resources – human, financial and otherwise – that you will need to develop and implement your sustainability programme with rough estimates of the time each person will need to dedicate to the programme

- What your competitors are doing

This provides you with the foundations of a sustainability programme and the information you will need to convince others to take action.

To the board

To get the resources you need you are going to have to convince the board, or at least most of the board. Unlike your other stakeholder groups, the board will be reasonably small so you have the opportunity to look at the individuals and their individual motivations – just expect them to be contradictory. On doing your research you may find you have a few people on your side from the very start, while others are a lost cause.

You may already have an advocate for sustainability on the board; if not, I suggest you find one. Who you choose will be affected by the personalities on the board and the issues affecting your business. Surprisingly, the board member with responsibility for sales is often keen on having a sustainability programme in place. They are often on the frontline, and are being asked by potential customers about the company's approach to sustainability. They are therefore keen to have an answer to these queries. If you're not sure if this is the case, ask people on the sales team.

Human Resources (HR) often hold responsibility for sustainability, particularly the community and employee aspects, while operations often hold responsibility for the environmental areas. Unsurprisingly, the economic aspects are generally being well managed within companies and are generally a strong focus.

Don't think that all your interactions have to happen within a specific meeting. Try speaking to board members one-to-one in more informal settings if possible, particularly potential advocates for sustainability.

When it comes to what will convince, with lots of boards this will just come down to one thing – the bottom line. How is this going to save or make the company money? This will be an easy sell for some aspects of your programme, but less clear for others. This is where it is key to be able to draw a strong link between your business, talk about the triple bottom line, and the benefits of a strategic approach to sustainability. If you use lots of energy, make that a focus; if increasing sales is a focus area, play up that aspect.

You are hopefully familiar with the company's mission and business development plan or strategy. How could any sustainability activities help deliver these things? If you can't think of any way your sustainability programme could deliver these things, I'd suggest you go back to the drawing board and think again.

Finally, what key issues is the business facing? What is your competition doing? Again make sure you include these in your plans, showing how sustainability can help deliver business success.

In summary:

- speak to board members individually and informally
- find an advocate on the board
- be prepared
- think about how a strategic approach to sustainability can benefit the bottom line
- tie your approach into the business strategy and risks

To key resource holders

So you've convinced the board – or they have put you up to this in the first place – but there are still people you will need to convince; as I said before, this isn't something that you can do on your own. And while Bob in operations might be very keen to help, Bob's boss may need convincing to give him the time needed for his role on the sustainability team.

So how do you convince these over-stretched, time-poor, middle or senior managers that it is a good idea to free up their equally stretched member of staff for the time that you need them?

- Think about how sustainability can enhance their role. Could your sustainability programme benefit them in any way – this could be by increasing the prestige of their department or role, increasing their budget or by making their job easier.

- How will becoming more sustainable benefit the business? They will probably be more interested in the strategic direction and the financial success of the business than the general workforce so explain the background to them.

- Details of the plan. You may not have all the details ironed out but you will need to have an idea of:

  - How much time you will require and for how long?

  - How will any lost resources be backfilled?

It is tempting to try and get all these people in one place at one time and convince them all at once, probably supported by a comprehensive deck of PowerPoint slides. That's probably easiest for you but is it for them?

Think about other possibilities. See them face-to-face if feasible or pick up the phone and have a chat – it's far more personal than being talked at for an hour or having an email land in your mailbox. Or think outside the box and send them a short video from a convinced board member or tweet them.

To key actors

Finally, you are putting together your sustainability team, but there is the chance that they are not the enthusiastic, committed bunch you hoped for.

The people you are including are in your facilities or site management team, HR, sales and purchasing. They are the people who will have to do something to embed sustainability in your business and will probably own parts of it, so you need them to be committed to it. They'll probably fall broadly into two camps – enthusiasts and sceptics.

The enthusiasts are easy to convince, in fact they may already be convinced. However, you may still need to set their minds at rest about workload – there is nothing more likely to quash enthusiasm than stress.

For sceptics, you may have the go-ahead but you will need to convince these people to put sustainability towards the top of their list and give their time and commitment to make it happen. How you approach this will depend on your company culture and the individuals involved, however, three areas to look at are:

- Empowerment – emphasise that this is an opportunity to shape and change things in the business. It is a chance for them to create their legacy within the company and to stand out.

- Trigger an epiphany – this may be a little hit-and-miss and isn't guaranteed to convert your sceptic, but it is a tactic used by a number of companies. At its simplest this could include showing your sustainability team a film such as Al Gore's *An Inconvenient Truth*, but could extend to getting an inspirational speaker to present to your team or taking a trip to a relevant destination.

- Targets – in many companies something isn't a priority until it is a formal target, particularly if employees receive performance-related bonuses. Use the systems that are currently in place to your advantage and ensure your sustainability strategy is part of team members' individual targets. Even if you don't include sustainability in formal performance targets have regular team meetings to track performance against targets. This helps keep sustainability on someone's list and encourages them to take action.

To your staff

You probably won't want or need to convince your general workforce at the very beginning. But further down the line you will want to let them know about your sustainability activities and maybe involve them, be it switching off lights, recycling or volunteering.

When trying to sell sustainability to your general workforce the best place to start is the altruistic side. Too much focus on the business benefits can seem cynical and can undermine the goodwill you wish to generate. That's not to say ignore them altogether – that depends to a large extent on your business culture – but they shouldn't be foremost in your communications.

It is also worth remembering that your employees probably understand what they do better than you do, and probably have ideas of their own to make improvements. So use them. Ask them for suggestions of what could be done differently or potentially not at all – you may find processes that are outdated or irrelevant. This won't just help move your sustainability strategy forward it will also lead to an engaged workforce.

QUESTIONS AND ACTIONS

- Who do you need to convince?

- Do you have any enthusiasts?

- What are the key issues affecting them – in general and relating to sustainability?

CHAPTER 6

Common Arguments

YOU MAY WELL MEET RESISTANCE to beginning your sustainability programme. Many of the arguments boil down to the same three issues – time, money and priorities.

Won't this take a lot of time?

There is no getting around the fact that developing and running a sustainability programme takes time. But everything does not have to be done at once. While you need to keep some momentum up, with such a broad initiative you need to focus your attention on specific areas and gradually broaden your scope. Obviously, it is possible to do everything at once but that requires resources which are generally out of reach for most businesses.

The second thing to consider is the benefits a sustainability programme will bring. It can help improve business resilience, reduce costs (see next sub-heading), increase sales, improve staff motivation and ensure legal compliance. The systems and processes you develop can help the efficient running of areas outside the scope of the sustainability programme. These benefits should pay for the time spent.

Won't this cost a lot?

There can be costs involved in developing and implementing a sustainability programme, particularly if you are looking to implement an accredited system. Capital investment is often required to improve resource efficiency or install renewables, but generally the payback on these is relatively short. Many savings can be made with minimal financial outlay.

In other areas such as training or community support, some investment is needed and, while the benefits are difficult to measure directly, will contribute to the efficiency of your business or in building the company's reputation.

Shouldn't we be focusing on the things that really matter?

There is an argument that sustainability isn't 'core' to the business and, as such, it isn't a priority area. It is an argument levelled at lots of business areas – IT, HR – but it is difficult to imagine a successful business that doesn't use any IT or employ any people.

I would also argue that sustainability is, by its very definition, core to the business when taking a long-term view. It is about making the business successful now as well as managing issues early and improving resilience to ensure the business remains successful.

Conclusion

A STRATEGIC APPROACH to sustainability recognises the reach of your organisation – the people and groups it affects and who affect it. It has the potential to bring a multitude of benefits, which include helping to:

- Manage risks and improve resilience

- Protect and build reputation

- Reduce costs and improve the efficiency of your operations

- Meet customer needs

- Motivate employees and attract new talent

- Ensure legal compliance

Reaping these benefits will take investment – of time and effort, if nothing else – from across the organisation. This means you will need to convince a wide variety of people that investing in sustainability is a good idea and will contribute the success of the business.

To do this you need to understand each group or individual's motivations and tailor your pitch to them. This isn't just what you say but how you say it, and thinking outside the box, or the meeting room, and talking to people in a way that works for them. Taking a busy person away from their day job to attend a largely irrelevant, full-day workshop isn't going to enamour you or the idea of sustainability to them.

CONCLUSION

This means doing some leg work and lots of preparation upfront to have the answers that your audience will want and need. This will include having some idea of the material issues affecting your business. You will want to revisit this when you have a team together so don't procrastinate about this; spend just long enough for you to identify the right people for the job, which, I realise, is easier said than done. To do this you need to look at:

- Your business and operations

- What people inside and outside your business think

- Risk areas

- Expenditure

- Any motivations for implementing a sustainability programme

- What your customers, suppliers and competitors are doing

- What your customers want

Use this information to build an idea of what you might actually do and what your sustainability programme may consist of. I have given some ideas and case studies but plenty more are available online (see Resources section).

Based on this, identify the resources you will need from around your business, possible capital expenditure and external help or expertise – not forgetting to look for any free support that may be available.

Don't forget to look at and ensure you understand your business, in particular the risks affecting it, the strategic direction, what it actually delivers to customers and why they choose your business.

All this preparation means that, when it comes to it, you should be ready and able to convince the relevant people.

Then there is just the small task of starting your journey by developing and implementing your sustainability programme... But in the long run your business, stakeholders and the environment will thank you for it.

....

Case Study – Yearsley Group

AS ONE OF THE LARGEST privately owned cold storage and distribution companies in the country, Yearsley Group works with some of the UK's best known food brands and stores as well as supplying public sector contracts.

They decided to implement a sustainability programme as they felt that not having one could put them at a disadvantage, especially in public sector tenders. This formed the basis of the argument to invest in developing a sustainability programme.

As the public sector was a focus area, Yearsley decided to implement an Environmental Management System (EMS) and certify it to the ISO 14001 standard. To add further credibility to their approach they used the ISO 26000 guidelines to inform their sustainability strategy and integrated the social aspects identified through this into the management system to give a combined Social and Environmental Management System (SEMS). This gave their approach and systems the credibility and assurance required by public sector and large private sector buyers.

In a busy, growing company like Yearsley time is always at a premium, so when the SEMS implementation stalled they engaged external expertise to give the process the momentum it needed.

Many of the material issues they identified as part of the implementation process were existing concerns such as electricity and fuel use and health and safety. Other areas were new, such as sourcing sustainable fish.

However, even for existing aspects the new framework gave a new perspective and renewed impetus. Actions ranged from installing solar panels and improving energy efficiency to developing a line of sustainable fish products.

It wasn't always an easy journey. The development and implementation of the SEMS took a lot of hard work and time, a scarce commodity in this thriving company. However, the hard work paid off and the systems quickly became routine.

Key to Yearsley's success was a committed team who understood the purpose of the programme and worked hard to implement the various parts. However, one of the biggest challenges was to keep sustainability near the top of a group of busy people's to-do lists. One solution to this was to hold regular team meetings to review targets, discuss progress and plan next steps. These regular check points – initially monthly and moving to quarterly – encourage team members to take action and make continuous improvements. Similarly, regular audits and an annual sustainability report help keep the programme at the forefront of people's minds.

As well as a committed team Yearsley have invested in capital projects and external help. The capital projects – such as solar panels – had clear payback periods which formed the basis of the business case for investment. The external consultancy included expertise to increase the efficiency of the cold stores, which had the knock-on effect of reducing costs and implementing the management system, which gave the process momentum and helped meet customers' needs.

....

Building a Business Case

The below provides a template for the high-level information you need to collect to build your sustainability business case, which is filled in here with data for an imagined widget manufacturer and delivery company.

STRATEGIC SUSTAINABILITY – BUSINESS CASE

Widget manufacturer and delivery company

....

KEY ISSUES FOR MY BUSINESS

Sustainability related:

- Large carbon footprint from energy use and travel miles
- Material wasted in production
- Health and safety of staff
- Source materials from politically unstable areas
- Relationship with neighbours – complaints regarding noise

Otherwise:

- Production costs
- Fuel costs

BUILDING A
BUSINESS CASE

- Health and safety
- Customers want to improve their product efficiency
- Winning tenders
- Production materials not always delivered in time

....

MATERIAL ISSUES

- Management system – certified
- Energy consumption
- Fuel consumption
- Waste materials in production
- Health and safety
- Supply chain
- Community investment
- Product development – increase efficiency in use and of materials in production

....

RESOURCES

Internal:

Representatives from: production team, distribution team, health and safety representative, procurement, communications

Capital:

Smart meters, new efficient widget polisher, improvement to site boundary to prevent noise travelling.

External:

Free resource efficiency survey

Who needs convincing	Motivations	How sceptical/ enthusiastic are they (1–10)?
MD	Cost, winning new business	6
Finance officer	Cost	4
Sales manager	Winning new business	9
Operations manager	Health and safety, delivering product on time	5
Distribution manager	Fuel efficiency, load-fill, driver hours and motivation	7

Resources

Beginner's guide on M4C website (registration needed) **http://www.m4c-sustainability.co.uk/educate.htm**

FAQs on M4C website **http://www.m4c-sustainability.co.uk/faqs.htm**

Business in the Community **http://www.bitc.org.uk/**

2degrees **http://www.2degreesnetwork.com/**

Groundwork **http://www.groundwork.org.uk/**

National Industrial Symbiosis Programme **http://www.nispnetwork.com/**

Sustainable Development Research Network Case Study Database **http://sdrncs.wordpress.com/**

Notes

1. UK: Young professionals who value corporate social responsibility higher than salary: www.mallenbaker.net/csr/CSRfiles/page.php?Story_ID=1881.

2. Sustainability is not only good business – it's a growth strategy: www.guardian.co.uk/sustainable-business/ibm-survey-consumer-behaviour?INTCMP=SRCH

3. Consumers are making sustainable choices, all they need is a little guidance: www.guardian.co.uk/sustainable-business/asda-sustainability-green-survey?INTCMP=SRCH

4. Primark: On the Rack: news.bbc.co.uk/1/hi/programmes/panorama/7461496.stm

5. Interface's Mission Zero: www.interfaceflor.co.uk/web/Sustainability/mission_zero

6. Walkers' carbon footprint: www.walkerscarbonfootprint.co.uk/walkers_carbon_footprint.html

7. SABMiller video – Respecting human rights. Why it's a priority for us and the action we're taking in Colombia and Honduras: www.sabmiller.com/index.asp?pageid=1035&year=2010

8. The Cadbury Story: 2008 – Cadbury Cocoa Partnership Launched: www.cadbury.co.uk/the-story#2000-Today

9. Manchester Airport Academy: www.airportacademy.co.uk/about.asp

10. Allianz Insurance – Community Support Programme: www.allianz.co.uk/home/about-allianz-insurance/social-responsibility/communities.html

For Product Safety Concerns and Information please contact our EU
representative GPSR@taylorandfrancis.com
Taylor & Francis Verlag GmbH, Kaufingerstraße 24, 80331 München, Germany

www.ingramcontent.com/pod-product-compliance
Ingram Content Group UK Ltd.
Pitfield, Milton Keynes, MK11 3LW, UK
UKHW040927180425
457613UK00011B/282